hardPressed Dual Poets Reader: Two

hardPressed Dual Poets Reader: Two

Linda Chown
David Miller

Published by hardPressed poetry, Ireland
http://hardpressedpoetry.blogspot.com/
hardpressedpoetry@gmail.com

to say thinking the blinding precision of dreams © Linda Chown 2017

Death of a Giraffe and other poems © David Miller 2017

This edition © hardPressed poetry 2017

ISBN: 978-1-872781-08-2

All rights reserved
No part of this publication may be reproduced in any form or by any means without prior permission of the publisher.

**to say thinking
the blinding precision of dreams**

Linda Chown

A Man Who Laughed in the Dark at Jackie Gleason

Daddy, this one's for you,
whimsical father marooned
in a sea of women.
You appear by heart-light
in the sheer pores of feeling.
You appear lean and indelible
stretched out at life like that from within.
Your blue eyes raging truth at the sky.

How we snickered like fools at you.
At your cane's tap tap clattering.
At your soundless chokings on food

in mid-afternoon deluxe restaurants.
Your eyes gasping about for help.
When Schatzki's ring kidnapped your throat.

How you got fixed sometimes
in a Victorian long-suffering,
fixed to pretend, to smile tolerant
in an eviscerating niceness.
Long you. Long suffering.

Badged in a dark-grey suit
pitched against the sky here
on a bare bridge in Grand Rapids.
Inside feeling burbled strong,
strong enough to burn the blue clamor
of your eyes into concrete pillars.

To shatter the still airs
and countermand finally
a long ingrown stillness:

To rage that truth of yours at the sky —
shedding passionate heart-light out
about us everywhere.

A Psalm for Cádiz

Death is in your peeling walls
Cádiz, in those skies that carry clouds
so lightly, in the cups of wine
and throat-wrenched songs in bars,
in the sinuous turnings of your dirty
streets. Death in the boats
that bring our pretty fish.
Death in the wind that swallows
our pretty words.
Death in the rats in our garbage

And you seem to take more of women.
You seem to eat their hearts out,
the biggest of them who come
to love you and your off beat ways
I hate the webs you sew:
One buried in the non-believer's graves,
nervous, wild-eyed woman, no friend
of mine, whose tiny taut bones
are rotting, nurtured by a
deaf Spanish gardener in the shade
of his days.
One a woman of spirit, of art,
my godmother by blood, a friend
at the end, who lost all her breathing
and her heart to lie adrift
in the dark she hated.
One a woman for beauty and grace
who's losing her energy and spirit
in this crumbling place.

Inevitable deaths and sickening, I
know, but there's something in your ways,
in those long 3000 years of fires
and plague and pillage that haunt,
that live in your unearthly winds
like buzzards fly, keeping even the tourists
away. Your walls must be made of bones

for all the buried here.
The fishes rich with English blood
still. The tide replete with long
lost wishes. So, when the wind sings
like it does today under the doors
I'm brought, premature, to dungeons
and morgues, to the sucklings of worms
and unperceived crumblings of earth.
I've come to despise your pride in the sea
rushing as it does over buried walls
and faces of an older Cádiz I'll never see.
I fear to never leave here,
to be taken by surprise
and blent into the background
with the wild sea birds singing
but a token song for me.

Death is in your walls, Cádiz,
in the faces of a people
who know the ocean always
closes around the forsaken places.

A Small Geography of Eternity

I.
At the edge of the forest
a beam of sunlight
strikes the field of redwoods.
Morning. The air clear,
smelling of pine needles
and oil. Camp fires burning.
I step over charred, heavy logs,
look into empty cabins,
and stare at their clean wood rooms.
No pictures hang on these walls.
The green wreath on that door
has gone limp forever.
A gunning of an engine.
The air still clear.

II.
The silence of the forest
surrounds me,
invisible,
the shape of a poem.

III.
More wood chips
settle into
the floor of this forest
than I ever can pick.

IV.
On the way home to San Francisco
I learn to take curves at 60 miles an hour.
I am near death
and what is eternity but
everything that is and
everything that is not around
me.

Annotations on a Jewish Theme

Please just for once let your hand go loose
and teach me what it is to watch the stars.

Take your body and sit into the chair
and show me how to bear confusion.

Let me learn what school can't give.
I am waiting for a mother's lessons,
to hear what you've been living for.

Just for once turn down that time
machine your brain has become.
No alarm is ringing now.

But to be near you is to hear
the wheels of worry click
through the wires of your mind
and I don't know why or what for.

Please let the world burn
again like it did once
in the family pictures
when your hair came back tight
behind your ears, long dark hair,
and you wore gypsy scarfs on your head
and looked ready to flirt.

You make me feel guilty.
Just for once don't be such a lady,
And let your fingers curl free
of the mind's hold:

these days with you
all I can hear
is the rattle
of its churning.

I walk about the streets
with my head half-cocked

seeing sideways like a sailor
long at sea, trying to make sense
of just what it is we must be

waiting for.

Newbie and

An old book news in me.
To write with a child's view.
There is more than everything to say.
Let the sun stay with summer language.
Let my tousled mind write to play

Another Easter in Conil

to Juan and Loli

At the end of March the sky
blues of a Matisse painting
hang on your white wall
and the sea suave and sleek
as guppy skin.
Roosters crow behind this house
in the dusty fields of Holy Thursday.
Church bells clang slow
as time gone under the years
of sinking sunsets
wiping this village's white face
clean of its deaths,
the lightning's flickering
passing and the wind's lonely sweep
across terraces clothed in laundry
while the harsh sighs of old ladies
bowed in black, thread the years
back and forth in a rhythm of red stitches
that stick to the walls,
the guts in the road
where one dead rooster lies
on his side, staring one-eyed
like the inevitable face of the sea.

As The Earth Turns about Love

The earth turns into the heat
it bends how you see
what you said about
love one afternoon when
sitting on a wood table
in the Granada light
after lunch and wine
noon cobblestones
a permanence of windows
things to look into

what you said about love
reminds you of mahogany
and the far edge of comets

Free Will in Spain

I stood on the corner of a wide boulevard
Where green taxis pulled at
The slow moving crowds.
The whole world turned black
On Good Friday night
And the resurrection
Just around the corner,
The people all ready,
The women veiled to death,
The men dressed up little boys,
The air so quiet you couldn't hear
The bells ringing,
The old gray church doors flung open,
And all around the block
A sober black procession.

Down in the subway alleys,
People scurried along the platforms,
Rushing for trains.
From all directions they came
In their best black clothes.
Moving with them, I
Pushed into a second class car
Between four short men,
Stood with them
In the smoke and the wet air.
Our street clothes wrinkled.
The whole car creaked.
The men pressed their slim thighs
Against me steady as drills.
Faces without glimmer or wink.
They just held tight to the arm straps,
Pressing.

The lights flickered.
The overhead fan squeaked.
There was no way out.
My hand reached
Out for the arm straps.

I felt a steady pushing
And the silence of people
Clinging together
Like bats taking off
In the dark.

One Night in Guecho

Layers. Layers and layers and layers
of lights in the small city.
At the top of a hill.
Guecho. On that street in Algorta.

Rough-faced land of Basques
stubborn in their silence,
singed with a kind of wild pride.

The white buildings
nestle large there together.
In the dark like glowworms.
shirred in their white skins.

Upstairs, aiming at the stars,
the quiet lights frazzle outwards
in the silent dim.

After the Heart Attack
> *the tie between us is very fine, but a Hair never dissolves*
>
> Emily Dickinson

Sometimes I drive myself crazy
imagining your blood, those silent red rivers.
Sometimes I'd like to go right through your skin
and know for sure that no jagged rocks
mar its even flow, that your channels
are wide and clear and clean, fit
for any worthy boat to sail away and go.
I would vacuum clean those veins for you.
I would build you dikes of polished stone.

But I can't come in. You're no toy doll
I can ever pull apart and know.
Your big heart beats behind awareness,
a thing no bloodtest can ever show.
For we sleep with faith, wake to a mystery
again and again and then pull words from us
like clams from reluctant shells,
spooning cold litanies of sound into morning streets.
I fear that no two hearts can ever meet.

But I would see you beat
those gray gamblers at their actuarial games
to live on beyond them,
to move across dying
like sunspots slither over the sun,
I would hear you sing in the bathroom
and watch you go at night to walk alone
and wake to take you to me,
to press that impermeable skin to me,
to lie curled up in a prosperous silence
where we can rock and share and smell
where we can warble a few of our offbeat tunes
until the underground rivers run wild
and put a stop to our splendid show.

        Conil

For Alison Krause
> *My sister bled to death for 45 minutes before an ambulance came, yet ambulances were available over the hill, reserved for guard and authority injuries only*
>
> --Laurel Krause

The girl who placed the stem   in a gun
Said I'm hit
And all the world burst
Into blood
As the bullet burrowed
And buried its cold metal
Thrust in living lungs.
And the world's TVs centered
The world's eye on
The rough shed minuet of death
On a campus lawn.
And later one said
What they said
With feeling,
Or built flimsy backgrounds
And gasped flatly.
But the fact remains
And gives more body to your name:
The moment perceiving
The violation of skin,
The way the invisible I is denied
And the heroic future
Disappears in an instant
Locking self in an eggshell
And everything you love
Darkened.

Her Green Dress

Once my mother made a dress.
From the beginning she made it
With one of those store bought jig-saw puzzle paper patterns.

It came out to be a stiff lime green
With severe shoulder pads.
Austere, just like the bun she wore
Which pulled her high cheek boned face
Back just too far to see her through.

My mother had her way of making things,
Of finishing beginnings.
It was a way she had of hearing—
Not just listening: it was a full court press hearing
Like a papal audience or gazing up at the stars awestruck in Hayden Planetarium.
Hers was that padded touch hearing which remembered,
Which held on long past overtime,
Stitching seams for us to live in beyond the chaos.

High Holy Day
Granada

The sun's light: conjunction
tight on brick wall.
To know they are church walls
Doesn't changes the sun
or its light, Greek light,
bright, turning inside out,
And do, the incense is not needed—
none of the props are…

The clue is in a vision,
a thing seen.
But somewhere long back when
after the great states fell,
visions took unlikely shapes
and we named those dark ages.

Birds always have nested
on the roof
of the oldest churches
even when icons screamed
terror and woe
while men hypnotized with hope
waited inside writhing.

This morning birds are chirping
and the sun moves slowly
over Sunday's ancient song
delivering us over
as it were
to the blue round of sky and space,
of angles and corners, touching,
color, and light fulfilling what it touches,
everywhere.

Homage to a Jamaican Stone Carver

He sat near the docks,
whittling his world into shape,
building horses from a heap of white stone.
Hunched on his heels, working,
he rarely looked up
to see the crowds of tipsy pink
ladies glancing down.

I saw on a pier smoking grass,
my own silk dress pink,
damp in the sun.
I found him against a wall
flanked with ten little horses
and silver shaping tools.
We looked briefly at each other.
His hands moved down, sculpting.
Soon, I, too, disappeared
leaving dark hands firmly on the reins
to adjust the dimensions of his world.

For far more
>   than
>   that
>   hour
those white horses he made
imaged through my high fogs.
And, even now, when of my own making,
I neglect the blueness of the bare sky,
the light he carved into permanent shape
glistens in my sight.

In Your Dark Look

in your dark look
it is as if those black braids
made you more solemn

inside there were no words
to pull out of those long thoughts,
that brooding in between

times when your music fingers
touching sound made you feel
closer to the holes
in the air maybe

the holes where harpists
mate the magic
in their music

where long thoughts turn liquid
and tease the starlight misty.

When the Blue Light Went Off
> *The uncertain meaning of yes. In a language spoken in words.*
> *Frances Jaffer*

Come full circle again
month by the clock
just in time to slide me in
and out of Italy again.

Slow train brought me here
and it rained and rained
and through the one slit eye
of my green old room
the blue light went off
out of the sky
and the buildings lay
in thin grey air
like a world of alley-cats
crying.

Who said it was
easy
before to me
to hang right into things?
to make blue from gray
with only desire to try on.

Come from a land
without winter
where cold doesn't seep in
so.
What do I know.

The lights fall
and wind
sweeps the ground
as months go round.
A slow trains coming
to take me back.

The sky sags meanwhile

like a puffy old man
dying.

                                        Brindisi, Italy

Making it So Easy to See

> *a kind of thinking, a mental complexion*
> Willa Cather

Upstairs in the study
two tall windows
whose blinds make it so easy to see
outside where the elms are busy
blowing fall around

on the green walls
black and white photos marking
old shapes of family feeling gone
in a dreadful unspoken eloquence

when once in San Francisco there was
this sense of endlessness
what I think of sometimes
as the dark blue airs of eternity
over the noisy silence of cities

that soundless explosion of now into the present
open as a small cloud puffing in flight
tugboats wild on the bay,
fog horns screeching deep beginnings

it was as it were life on the run, all that feeling
under wraps, under odd wool caps, in the brightest light.
life going on like a broken kaleidoscope, like that over and over
when now I remember being clearly cloudy
being unhatched in blue light. Waiting for everything
quietly blinking and soaking myself into that gigantic Pacific
life was as my own private light show in the day in the night
a kaleidoscope of windows just about to open
the air was so still

On the hills, here and there, a massing of tired buildings

On Looking She Was

On looking she was. Always
Staring as though there were
Depths and hollows to see through
Into. Something to stay with her
little girl hands twisting
She would try to pull the world intro her musical fingers
To play the sound close,
She was just always so oblivious
Of her difference
they knew her for the witch
That she was Juden commie sick girl

The dark twins Cassie and Lassie knew what to do with her kind
From behind they lassoed the tip of her braid
And soaked it dark and silent in an inkwell.
She kept her still
Her brooding eyes set inside in a look

Little girl out on the edges
No howdy doody times for you.
You were to gaze hard looking up
Beyond the puppet land of the fabulous fifties
You were to come home to hide behind the sound.

All her time life opened up in a river for her
To cry through

On Reading Old Poems
> *...if you do not even understand what words say,*
> *how can you expect to pass judgement on what words conceal?"*
> H.D.

Surprised by all those words,
the barren complications, by the way
I tried too hard to make things more,
yes, say it out, to be creative,
I must have been living indoors too long,
my eyes peering through tree leaves,
my nose breathing old book dust,
tongue lacquered with liquidy discretions
so that these poems seem mummies
in a glass cage, all wrapped and wound,
yellowing at the seams, too suspect of fraud
to be the fertile that poems need be, to be.

I would have them leaves, transparent
in the light. I would grow them green
to catch the sight. Their sound ring
like colored bead doors swaying in a village
wind at night. I would let them go like children
or bubbles in the air, convinced of their shape,
if I knew they really came from feeling,
where animals quake. We'd join
and climb, threading words on the sky
and disperse like summer fireworks,
bright and spent in an unrepeatable fall,
hailing down a small touch of glory,
giving our all.

Passing Salt Flats in San Fernando, Spain

Strange to be reminded of Japanese
men, of watercolor films tidy
as a plane's eye's view:
squares, vaguely green and brown
patches and wiry men
padding, barefooted in loose pants
and wide-brimmed hats
over the salt field's flats.
They are hoeing salt
from the land's pockets
here on the edge of Europe
which the full tide has filled.

Regal this like a coronation
in its form and I remember more
of the Japanese woman
drawing water, of the monk's
purposefully shaved head and towns
of dark wood and mats of straw,
towns whose paper walls
open into light
like a quiet maze of rivers.

But here, now, the bus races
like a fool through history
past the mud flats and whitewashed shacks,
bouncing and heaving on the narrow road,
its glass eyes glittering
greedy to arrive
while just outside
the sun is high
and the world suddenly old and silent.
A chorus of men digging their toes
into earth and the salt seems to quiver
in the wind with all the beauty that can be
on the road of San Fernando.

Brought up to Music

> *I mean music that makes the mind*
> *Continue in the move of melody*
> Francis Hosman

Brought up to music,
brought up to listen,
and hear harder,
the walls hanging violins,
lush in their brown wood,
brought up in sound and tone
and pitch, volume and melody,
playing music, I was on a sound track,
a straight line right into
the moment, daily mainlining the present,
brought up to music
and touching the world into shape
through the tips of my polygraphic fingers.

Rinny: In the Beginning

> *For though I'm small, I know many things,*
> *And my body is an endless eye*
> *Through which I know everything*
> Gloria Fuentes, "Now"

In a bright time.
She was. A fervor in the wind.
One of those quiet fires in the stillness.
It was in her eyes.
Their dark wine drops
Raging in the school halls
Those shiny metal lockers.

Her seething eyes.
Premature
In that copious solitude.

To an Unknown Painter

In the picture the two monks pose
against sharp grey cliffs,
their white robes full as Renoir women.
The gentle spread of linen
almost avoids the pain contained
in the wounds sustained
where a knife blade cleaves
into one monk's head,
sticking snug as an ax in wood
and where the arrow plunged
in the other's heart
stringing his guts
into beads of pain.

Still the two men pose
bucolic in that painter's eye
with a trace of joy flush
in their cheeks

There must have been a light for him
To leave those spoiled old monks
so bloodless
or he knew already
how the end would come
and left their blood alone
and all the rituals of pain
to keep a light for centuries
on those pale and willing men.

Ubrique, Spain

Beginning to feel. Where it
was. As the sky fell in the far.
A dabble of chives set to rise
green and tarragon wisps
wanding about on that breeze.
Pollen clumps settle
where it was beginning. To feel
in the far white
honeycomb houses
in the mountain villages
burn mystical
in a rage of sunlight

What She Thought She Saw

She heard the rainfall
And felt the water spatter
She wrote much of the leaves
Changing as they do
Wrote so much of what she thought
She saw — she thought she saw
Things beginning again and over
Life as a round circle in the sun
Change as a copper wheel turning
In the rain she hears the bird-sounds
She saw no light moving it was so quiet
She was left with the leaves,
Just the leaves in her kind of silence
The peace you had to fight to preserve
The place that makes the sounding stronger

Writing to

> *I tie knots in the strings of my spirit*
> *to remember*
> *Jack Gilbert*

Write to. Write about not.
It just begins. And she does.
Little all in her combat.
Not about. But write to
Her troubled eyes.
Close to get. Come to see
The fire raging in the quiet.

In a brood she was
Turned outside to stay in,
Playing with her suspenders
In Cousin Belle's house in the city,
Violins pressed to the walls and Gonnie
Staunch there, braiding her exploding hair.

Only the lonely, little in bay windows,
With special keys of solitude,
Tell stories with their fingers,
Plucking passions in the sunset.

Wood Sight

> *you have to be rooted in something tangible*
> *if you wish to dream in peace*
> Terrance Hayes

I.
When you went gone bye
I bought you wood:
Hairless paupers squirmed in the sun;
A gray mare hoof-huffed, pawing at the dust;
One alabaster finch frozen in night fright
rocks speechless in mid-flight.
A mint shadow of the moon awakens
and spreads a shell husk-sliver green—

The sky burst open and rivers pitch-black
jostle, bleeding vertical and ragged in the skyline-
Pandemonium spreading across the foreparts-
A tumult of silent sparrows floats
upwards, wings opening into a tempest—
mysterious impulse poised on blind morning brick.
Patchy pieces of green pinplode in the air,
sharp like seasonal sparkles, drifting dim downward .
All the lead gaskets ever soldered gyre-wipe
shapeless pockets of acrid air into a light
far too saturated now to see.

II
Once, roasted smug, blind in sunlit oblivion
I would have built a kind of trap
to keep you, I would have, a shiny locket
of a thing, safe, secluded, shelter-away sham ,
The shrill shame of it, hard, smooth, impervious, prison rig,
away from those quixotic currents fluid and fluent.

After the time when you went gone bye
after the shadow of the moon awoke
the hairless paupers who squinted
into the burning-acrid morning
And I bought you wood--
not just any old wood to hold you,

I wanted to meet you head-on in the deep,
to build something infinitely far beyond sturdy—
something to grow into, to endure
beyond before because.

III
That baroque morning, I bought you wood,
touched the porous resinous cellular
graininess of it, the gnarls and knots, bulbs and sweet chips,
perspicuous patinas and flaunting figures,
the very sap of it grows soft, dusty and natural in the seeing.
Touching two matching side-tables,
one by each in sheer tactile deference,
their drawers sliding open cobbled, unique.
I grew there like a sapling rooted at long last,
rooted and bound free in my origins.
Slathered in such diffusion of wood sight,
suffusion of sycamore and rosewood
curly cherry and ash-cottage oak—

The world begins simply to spin, slow, long, textured,
grainy and porous in my eyes touching.
On a morning of hairless paupers and alabaster
finches rocking speechless in mid-flight
I went out a closed door, past gray walls and steel-magenta
dikes
and bought you all the wood I could fit
in a fast flipper-flopper of a heartbeat
and fastened it all free in its origins:
braided, branded, burned in this solemn wood vision,
sweet lullaby of stillness, apocalyptic morning bright,
all the way open metaphysical treat,
being here now for all the now there is.

Cherished alchemy just come upon
the morning you went gone bye
and I bought you wood all grainy and porous
to be here for now where the world begins to spin
and shiver sweetly in its consonance,
soft in wood-inflected light

Women Need to Be Respected

to write moonlight,

to drink orgies,

to proliferate,

to be still as stones,

to kick stars,

to caress peach pulp,

to be celibate as sunburn and

fanciful as fairy dust.

Words and Bees at the Marina
>*How can we live without the unknown before us?*
>René Char

in the sun again
at the Marina we were
new and hot glowing
in the mystery of potential
body to body we were still
standing hot when you said
there cold in the light
when you said that
my body wide open to you
feeling ready there
glowing with you
green round trees sweet
pressing the blue
we had made a place for ourselves
there to float when you said:
I was not finished, not complete.

like a bee Id been sapping seeping
honey coating sugar skin sublime
I needed you said more: my own
philosophy of life to live with

My body humming double dahlias
My soul throbbed eloquent now to know
My brain writing a fertilized elegance

You said I needed something. Of a philosophy.
to have. about life. later.
to know about it to know, a philosophy.

Those words stick the wind. Still.
Gray pawns in rich air.
Just when I was glowing
honey coating sugar skin.
Bee talk saturated busy. I be
actually wild in this mystery of potential.
Word talk fast-froze the wind

still, Whip-lashed it to.

In the sun there that day at the Marina
when we were all new and hot
glowing out with ourselves.

How Where We Were Was
> *Love allows us to walk in the sweet music of our particular heart*
> Jack Gilbert

On the street where you lived
we bought a house without the roots
you hated those false forever knots
and wanted to keep us stars in the trees
on the street where we lived
you made mulch and turned honey golden

and I surrounded us with flowers
and dried the herbs and seasonings of our summers
where we were, there, complete, in a love beyond the saying
as a music of smoky sounds, tenor sax bleeding
the whole tones of us making a love beyond words
to say for what I loved about your face. Holiday birds we thrived
in a green room. Half-moons rising in our eyes
sudden like solid smoke. On that street where we lived
together like stars in the trees. Such a singing without song-sound.

Two refugees planting each other fresh in the air.
A hoe-line could have not sown them any surer.
Strange star roots in the open. Once you said we
knew paradise. Just like that. A paradise. Star roots we were
surely, free to spread about with the honey and all those roses.

Some Times Writing

Sometimes writing in the rain
I hear the quiet people
Whispering dream
Memories.

Red husks of memory.
A violence of fragments.

All that they wanted.
All that mattered.
Dream timing in a sequence--
Echoes and silhouette and heartbreak.
As one sometimes,
As we, are, some times,
Writing in the rain.

When Seeing Beyond Yourself

to Oliver Sacks for everything

you are just what you were then
when you used to stare at those fillies
flicking fly-thick tails
in a California twilight
your dark eyes spokes then
just as you are now trying to see
beyond yourself as we do
when we get blind and baffled

They Say I Write Like a Woman

They say I write like a woman,
They say I write little.
I say I spit feathers and blood.
The doorway of death
The chastity of forever love

To Be or To Be

It is impossible
to be all
that we would like
to be, dream
to be

It is in our reach
to take hope off
its soft sad pedestal

and in the grind of our minds
wrench ourselves back
into this one chance
always present

Missing

I
How long it was, that night.
The birds on the block
cackling and hooing till daylight,
fire trucks screaming in the city,
whining and whistling through
every corner of the bed
I tried to rest in.
And Herman, the huge crazy black Afghan
next door, looney too-
He heard the wild sounds,
bayed madly at the moon
in his highest dog croon
while I dipped against the bed,
choking out sleep,
listening to the whoosh of cars in the street.

Are you dead, I said.
Did you fall off a cliff
and land on a beach
somewhere on a walk you took?
Did you take off with someone
or did you just take off?

My knees tighten together.
I am shaking, smoking.
I am in the middle of night.
Where are you?

II
Running downstairs calling you.
6 AM. I fall off a cliff,
landing alone at the bottom
of the stairs in a morning light
pale blue and moist,
the color and taste of dawn.
The light is too gentle
for this violent surprise.
Alone in my time now?

I really don't know.
Don't know what to do with myself
now. My time is passing. Fast.
The daylight's coming,
exposing every hard surface in the house.
Every thing in place.
Herman sleeping on the lawn.
A perfect quiet morning.
No evidence you are not here.

I must be in hell,
I am hell.
The world has stopped for me.

My terrible waiting.

III
When I got the policeman on the phone
he said how long has he been missing
how long   been missing
he said
we'll issue a routine search
what is your name he said
these things
so formally.
I said don't think
I will do that now.

IV.
You are the only
person in the world
I could tell
you are dead to.

V
I take a window seat
on the bus going downtown
to meet you.
Here and there.
People amble in the heat.

The broken leather seat I lean on.
Attention. At ease.
Attention. At ease.
The wind begins to blow
from light to light
down Market Street.

Your gray tweed jacket
brushes me, scratching
stab of memory
There is one of you and one of me.
One of me and one of you.
Together still makes two.

VI
You stayed in a hotel
to be away from me,
to be, for I was missing.
Sitting together
in the Chinese restaurant
all the questions
I would have asked you
are for me.

We eat lightly.
I have not been
the keeper of my cabin.
My terrible waiting.

My mind turns on itself.
A bowl of soup,
an old scratch of a poem.
Your gray jacket
brushing on my hair.

The wind rustles the papers in the street,
inevitable, bitter-sweet,
my love,
growing.

Meeting

I
Almost out the door, I saw you
headed for the other wing of the building.
We were only one courtyard apart.
I had not seen you for months,
could have left safely,
pretended you were not around.
I watched you move, forward,
surely in a new blue suit,
dark glasses over your eyes.
My mind churned.
If I went now, no one would know.
But you are getting older.
Suddenly I ran across the courtyard.
Holding on tight to my books and purse,
I ran to meet you.

II
Daddy, I try to tell you
and I fail.
I try to tell you
guts are personal.
They don't always show.
I tell you I'm different now,
and you wanting to know what that means
say, well, how to do you feel about life?
Then I can't begin to tell you anything.
I don't want to know anymore.

Daddy, I'm not a political radical
and you're disappointed.
I even made a joke of being Camus' stranger
but it wasn't funny.
Neither of us laughed.

You asked me where my passion went.
How can I tell you that?

    Daddy, I've talked myself out

all my life
with words.

        I'm engaged to a new silence.
The rules are simple.
Say just what you believe,
don't say just anything.
Believe me.
I'm not saying I'm holy.
I'm still afraid of my voice.
But hear me. Hear me now.
Daddy, hear my voice.

You lean across the bench in the courtyard
and give me a fast kiss on the cheek.
I watch you move away,
your briefcase heavy with books,
you on your way to work
and I on my way to it,
I watch you go away,
your steps slower this time.
What more can we say, now, Daddy.

III
On the bus going home
I listen for myself,
checking to see
how truthful I am,
checking to see
how I am.

The Trip
On LSD

the Marin suburbs on Sunday
wasted, buried
under telephone lines.
Vision shoots
jagged across the highway—
poles stick out of my eyes.

      My cigarettes, purple—
smoke like a joke
and the car he drives
an old-time movie scene.

Everything pushed out of us
to watch for.

Brain Drops

> *And the rain is brain-colored*
> *Stan Rice*

And suddenly the street people
On fire, their bone-backs arch,
Stretching into cold air.
Like orange live wires
Broiling the night
Wet

Fervent spectacle of brain drops,
Sky-scopes of spider writing.
Burnt alchemies curving in.
Sheets of golden marrow
Hover, spinning
Perpendicular.

Translucent sparks
Of brain paste flicker
Splendid tawny—
Writing rain articulate across urgent sky.

A day they say to remember

It's Memorial Day again,
a day they say to remember
those missing in action
remember missing those
long blue sky sailor stripes
remember your father in action
when you were little remember the Marne
and he was in action burning the brush
fire mixed black soot on white
fog drifts remember when you were
little with that big frown
and your mother sat there waiting
pulling down on her red skirt

DEATH OF A GIRAFFE
and other poems

David Miller

A few of these poems have previously appeared in *Poetry Salzburg Review* and *STRIDE*.

The quotation "Measured outlines, like footprints, have no point of view" is taken from Massimo Scolari, *Oblique Drawing: A History of Anti-Perspective.*

Starting From a Photograph by Diane Arbus

I encountered her in the park, a tough-looking young woman smoking a cigar; she had cropped blonde hair, and the glazed eyes of a drug addict: or so it seemed. She obligingly posed for my camera; but she still scared the shit out of me.

Oblique.

'No, I turned myself in', she said; 'I didn't want it hanging over me at Christmas. What was it about? – just getting into an argument with some fucking idiot.'

Direct: you might say so; in some respects. Not so much face-to-face: more face-at-face.

A cutpurse? Possibly. Two shadows to one person, simultaneously thrown by a single sun.

Coming across an elderly woman harassed by an Alsatian dog, she punched the animal in the face.

Urban and industrial panoramas squeezed and further squeezed: elongated buildings (silos; tenements; high-rise hotels), pushed towards and against each other. Wire fences. Barbed.

Where she lives:

There's a window box, with geraniums; a toy bird, singing; a spider in the bathroom; a cracked wine glass. And a yellow-ochre sky in view.

She encountered a scholar; a scholar lost to himself. A scholar of what? he wondered.

She might lift her hand or not, smoke or not, turn or not, pose or not, leave the park and re-enter it, light a cigar, pose and then pose again. She might pursue herself, flee herself, pass herself and continue or come back.

'We may eat cubs if we think they were sired by another male, but we're not barbarians', said a lion in her dream.

She pursues, and is pursued.

In soldierly perspective. Towers; fortifications: open to the corporeal eye, via the mind's eye. *Measured outlines, like footprints, have no point of view.*

A star, six-pointed, formed the top of the tower, poised at the heavens; echoed in shape by surrounding walls.

Long range missiles, suicide aircraft strikes. Then artillery fire.

Walls, in ruins: rubble.

Her form ebbs and flows, strengthens and fades.

Landscapes withered, bleached, blasted: etiolated here, burnt and blackened there.

Black. A red edge. Fire. Stone; rocks.

Echo.

Or, finally, nothing to echo.

Clarinet

A clarinettist plays and dreams... dreams and plays: what else should he (or she) do?

Until a tiny spider crawled its way into the clarinet and made its home there, chewing the pad beneath a key and also laying its eggs.

The bottom notes, most dearly prized, rendered unplayable.

Then he (or she) could only dream.

Bali, 1930s/40s

long into the night
gamelan music sounding
to cheer the prisoner
keeping him company
painter photographer
homosexual
predator?
interned on the island
....
riding in carriages
pulled by the poor
lady anthropologist
's breakdown
trance her subject
all to a point of no
return
....
and his death at sea
after another internment
and deportation
ghostly repetitions
under moonlight
ordinary and monstrous

East London, 1975

his long hair pulled
and stones and glass
thrown by children
at the young stranger
in the street at night
....
clutching his clarinet case
for dear life

Bushfires (I)

Fires set

then sit

then run

Bushfires (II)

— My ear fur and paws
your beak and feathers

burnt

Bushfires (III)

The animals turn back
as the smoke thickens

Death of a Giraffe

Blood spurts from the long neck
and the long legs give way

Air Rifle

A shot to its eye
a shot to its side

(yet the cat may live)

The Pencil of Nature
(after Fox Talbot)

These are the sun-pictures themselves
and not
en-
grav-
ings
in im-
itation

Dew still there?
or else rain
earlier in the day:
after putting out food
for the birds
slippers and trouser ends soaked

Honeycomb, waffles, pancakes with syrup. Strong coffee with milk.

A barque. Or a catafalque.
From exile and into exile: we are born, live and die, exilic.
And strive to be ethical.
— That day promised much; but the sky and the sea darkened...
and then all was lost.
A lock of ash-blonde hair.

(for Robinson Jeffers)

your hand writes
my hand writes

ghost hand writes

in
the

blue

blue

blue

Fields of Ash

ash	ash	ash	ash
sadism	ash	ash	ash
murder	ash	ash	ash
genocide	ash	ash	ash

Linda Chown was born in Berkeley and was an Intellectual History Major at the University of California, in that city during the 1960s events at Berkeley which suffused her with hope about the potential for human improvement and unity. After a year-long trip to Europe, she worked at the San Francisco Poetry Center at the time of the Howl Trial and the regular readings of Ginsberg, Creeley, and others. As a student in the mingled Creative Writing, English MA of that time, she studied Chaucer, John Donne, Shakespeare, Samuel Johnson, William Carlos Williams and Charles Olson at the same time as participating in scheduling and listening to weekly poetry readings, and giving readings of her own poetry. She then lived in Spain for some 11 years, teaching with the University of Maryland before returning to University of Washington where she got a doctorate in Comparative Literature. Since then she has lived and worked in Michigan.

David Miller was born in Melbourne (Australia) in 1950, and has lived in London (UK) since 1972. His more recent publications include *The Dorothy and Benno Stories* (Reality Street Editions, 2005), *In the Shop of Nothing: New and Selected Poems* (Harbor Mountain Press, 2007), *Black, Grey and White: A Book of Visual Sonnets* (Veer Books, 2011) and *Reassembling Still: Collected Poems* (Shearsman, 2014). He has compiled *British Poetry Magazines 1914-2000: A History and Bibliography of 'Little Magazines'* (with Richard Price, The British Library / Oak Knoll Press, 2006) and edited *The Lariat and Other Writings* by Jaime de Angulo (Counterpoint, 2009) and The *Alchemist's Mind: a book of narrative prose by poets* (Reality Street, 2012). He is also a musician and a member of the Frog Peak Music collective. His most recent publication is *Spiritual Letters*, published by Contraband Books in 2017. He is not a Professor of Sociology, despite reports to the contrary.

www.ingramcontent.com/pod-product-compliance
Lightning Source LLC
Chambersburg PA
CBHW020021050426
42450CB00005B/578